WILD WHEELS!

Hottest Sports Cars

By Bob Woods

Enslow Publishers, Inc.
40 Industrial Road
Box 398
Berkeley Heights, NJ 07922
USA

http://www.enslow.com

Library of Congress Cataloging-in-Publication Data

Woods, Bob.
  Hottest sports cars / Bob Woods.
    p. cm. — (Wild wheels!)
  Summary: "Learn about some of the world's most famous sports cars; how they began,
and where they are going in the future"—Provided by publisher.
  Includes bibliographical references and index.
  ISBN-13: 978-0-7660-2873-9
  ISBN-10: 0-7660-2873-9
  1. Sports cars—Juvenile literature. I. Title.
  TL236.W66 2008
  629.222'1—dc22

                                    2007007428

Printed in the United States of America

10 9 8 7 6 5 4 3 2 1

To Our Readers:
We have done our best to make sure that all Internet Addresses in this book were
active and appropriate when we went to press. However, the author and publisher have
no control over and assume no liability for the material available on those Internet sites
or on other Web sites they may link to. Any comments or suggestions can be sent by
e-mail to comments@enslow.com or to the address on the back cover.

Cover Photo: Alamy/Transtock Inc./Guy Spangenberg **Back Cover:** Alamy/Mark
Scheuern
Interior Photos: Alamy/imagebroker, p. 9; Alamy/Motoring Picture Library, pp. 3, 11,
23 (middle left), 36, 42–43; Alamy/Colin Woodbridge, p. 13; Alamy/Phil Talbot, pp. 1, 3,
5, 19, 22 (middle and bottom); Alamy/Al Satterwhite, p. 21; Alamy/Adrian Sherrat, p. 23
(middle right); Alamy/Bob Masters Classic Car Images, pp.1, 23 (bottom), 26, 41;
Alamy/Alvey and Towers Picture Library, p. 4; Alamy/Helene Rodgers, p. 32; Alamy/
www.gerardbrown.co.uk, pp. 3, 27; Alamy/Paul Collis, pp. 3, 34; Alamy/Transtock Inc.,
pp. 28, 37; Alamy/Mark Scheuern, p. 43; Alamy/Jack Sullivan, p. 23 (top right);
Associated Press/AP, p. 31; AP/Gabriela Noris, p. 6; AP/Plinio Lepri, p. 12; AP/Marco
Vasini, p. 10; AP/Anja Niedringhaus, p. 14; AP/Martial Trezzini, p. 17; AP/Donald
Stampfli, pp. 1, 18; AP/Marta Lavandier, p. 35; Corbis/Carculture, p. 39; Jeffrey Dean,
Tucson, AZ, p. 29; Getty Images/Scott Barbour, p. 24; iStockphoto, p. 22 (top left).

Contents

The Wheel World

We humans are always on the go. And we often like to go fast. That explains why people love cars—especially fast ones! But speed is just one reason why people love Ferraris, Porsches, and other foreign sports cars. From bumper to bumper, inside and out, these cars are marvels of modern engineering and styling.

America has also built its fair share of fast, sporty, powerful, good-looking, and well-built automobiles. The Dodge Charger,

Ford Mustang, Pontiac GTO, and Chevy Camaro were big hits during the 1960s and 1970s. In fact, modern versions of each are now being produced. And Chevy's Corvette has ruled the American road as the nation's one and only true sports car since 1953. However, when a bright yellow Lamborghini Murciélago pulls up, no one can help but stop and stare at that Italian beauty.

Cars are manufactured in dozens of different countries, but ones built in Italy, Germany, and Great Britain hold a special place in many car lovers' hearts. For decades, Lamborghini, Ferrari, Porsche, BMW, and Jaguar have put some of the hottest models ever made on the road.

The Chevy Corvette is considered by many to be America's only true sports car. This is a classic 1969 Sting Ray model.

FINISH LINE

CHAPTER 1

Italian Stallion: Ferrari

This was no ordinary test drive of a new car. It was an 84-day, 20,000-mile spin around two continents.

The people at Ferrari needed to check out their latest supercar—the 2007 12-cylinder 599 GTB Fiorano. This "test drive" was a special event called the Pan-Am 20,000. The long journey began on August 24, 2006, in Belo Horizonte, Brazil, and ended in New York City nearly three months later, on November 17.

A team of 48 journalists from the top car magazines in the world took turns driving two 599 GTB Fioranos (one red, one blue) through 16 countries in South, Central, and North America. The drivers took the cars over mountain roads, through tropical rain forests, across scorching deserts, down interstate highways, and finally onto the busy streets of New York City. Along the route, people stopped and stared at these hot-looking cars.

To go along with its good looks, a 599 GTB Fiorano, fully loaded with options, has a huge price tag. How huge? Around $275,000! (Compare that with a new Chevy Malibu, a midsize American family car, for about $18,000.) So what, exactly, do you get for more than a quarter of a million dollars?

You get a beautifully sculpted car designed to slice through the air like a rocket ship on four wheels. There are leather seats to sink into, a killer sound system to groove to, and a navigation system to get you where you are going. The 599's ride is ultra-comfortable. It steers easily through sharp curves, and high-tech brakes stop it on a dime. While other expensive cars have many of the same features, none has a 12-cylinder engine quite the same as this car's.

Start it up, and the 599 blasts off from a standstill to 60 miles per hour (mph) in about three and a half seconds. It will reach its top speed of 205 mph in 11 seconds.

WILD FACT

A cylinder is a space inside an engine that contains a piston, valves, and other moving parts. These parts supply power to the transmission, which turns the front, rear, or all the wheels of the vehicle, depending on the car.

The words "speed" and "Ferrari" have gone together ever since the company was started in Italy by Enzo Ferrari in 1945.

During the 1950s and 1960s, Ferrari focused on producing race cars. The company did not make many street cars. Every one it did produce, however, was hand-made. These street versions were very expensive.

The Ferrari symbol is recognized around the world.

Over the years, Ferrari has continued to make high-priced, high-performance masterpieces. In the 1970s, the Daytona was a sleek, ultra-fast model usually owned by millionaires. It earned its name from Ferrari's success at the 24 Hours of Daytona endurance race held in Florida.

Ferraris became hot in American pop culture in the 1980s when Tom Selleck, the star of popular TV detective show *Magnum P.I.,* chased criminals around Hawaii in his red Ferrari 308 GTS every week. Not to be outdone, the cool crime-stopping duo on

The Red Baron

Michael Schumacher drives his Ferrari Formula One race car in 2006.

The Ferrari racing team has had decades of success in Formula One racing. Formula One is a category of international auto racing in which specially built cars compete in events at tracks around the world for championships each year.

Sixty-eight different drivers have raced for the Ferrari team in Formula One. The king of them all is Michael Schumacher of Germany. Schumacher joined the Ferrari team in 1996. He became known as the "Red Baron," after a famous German fighter pilot from World War I, and also for the red Ferrari he drove at speeds up to 220 mph. In 2000, he won the first championship for Ferrari since 1979. He went on to capture four more back-to-back driver and constructor championships before retiring in 2006.

During his remarkable Formula One career, Schumacher set many records. They include most championships (seven), most championships in a row (five), most wins (91), and most wins (72) for one team—Ferrari.

Miami Vice caught up with lawbreakers in their Ferrari Testarossa. Both Ferrari models became popular in the United States.

To celebrate its 50th anniversary in 1995, Ferrari introduced the 12-cylinder, 520 horsepower (hp) F50. Only 349 of the supercars were manufactured, because, the company stated, "Ferraris are something cultural, a monument. They must be hard to find." They were pretty tough to afford, too, at a price today of at least $500,000!

Today, along with the 599 GTB Fiorano, Ferrari also offers several other street models. One is the 612 Scaglietti. It has a V-12 engine and four seats. (A V-12 engine is a

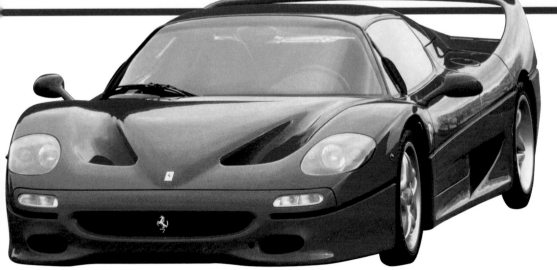

1996 Ferrari F50

A Ferrari official poses next to the one-of-a-kind Ferrari 375 MM. It was built in 1954 for the actress Ingrid Bergman.

12-cylinder engine with two sets of six cylinders each, lined up alongside each other in a "V" shape.) This car is designed to look like a Ferrari that was custom-made in 1954 for Ingrid Bergman, a popular actress. It was called the 375 MM, and Bergman's was the only one built.

On all five continents, Ferrari and its prancing horse emblem have become symbols of supercars for the super rich. When the company tests a new model in a 20,000-mile marathon, though, owners can be sure that their money is well spent.

Ferrari has used its racing experience and the latest technology to develop one of the fastest and most exciting and exotic cars ever made—the FXX. But even if you could afford the huge price tag of nearly $1.9 million, you still could not just drive away in your amazing new car.

The company has built only 30 of these very special cars, and they have all been sold to past Ferrari owners. For the first two years, each owner is required to drive the car on a closed track in Italy, on special days organized by Ferrari. Afterward, they must let Ferrari know how the supercar performed. Owners can also have private track sessions. The FXX is not designed to drive on public roads.

The racy-looking FXX has a V–12 engine that can kick out 800 hp. Shifting through its six–speed transmission, it can reach speeds of nearly 200 mph. And for safety's sake, your very own race car comes with a racing helmet, suit, gloves, and shoes.

The Ferrari FXX

CHAPTER 2

Raging Bull: Lamborghini

Kobe Bryant was excited about surprising his wife, Vanessa, with a brand-new car. Bryant is the superstar shooting guard for the Los Angeles Lakers and owner of three National Basketball Association (NBA) championship rings (2000, 2001, and 2002). As one of the highest paid players in the

NBA, he would not be expected to buy just any wheels for Mrs. Bryant. In fact, in 2001 he bought her one of the fastest—and most expensive—cars in the world. It was a Lamborghini Murciélago. But still, the car was not quite right.

It had nothing to do with the two-door supercar's awesome looks. Hand built at the Automobili-Lamborghini factory just outside of Bologna, Italy, the ultra-sleek, bright yellow Murciélago sat low to the ground. It featured Lamborghini's special "scissor" doors (they lift upward, toward the front of the car, not outward like most doors). Vanessa could not complain about the V-12 engine, which could easily rocket the car along at 200 mph. So what was wrong?

It seems that she had never driven a car with a stick shift. The Murciélago only comes with a six-speed stick shift. So the car was customized with an automatic transmission, which changes gears on its own. This made the Bryants' Murciélago the only one of its kind in the world. The final price tag: $400,000!

The company that makes these luxurious vehicles was founded in 1963 by Ferruccio Lamborghini. He was a wealthy businessman who earned his fortune by

WILD FACT

"Stick shift" is another name for a manual or standard transmission, which requires the driver to change gears by hand, using a foot-operated clutch.

building slow-moving farm tractors. Away from the office, he enjoyed driving very fast-moving cars. But he always complained that the clutch on his Ferrari 250 GT did not work well. Lamborghini took his complaint straight to the top, all the way to owner Enzo Ferrari. As the story goes, Ferrari told Lamborghini to stick with driving tractors—in other words, to "buzz off"!

Instead, Lamborghini went home and started his own car company. His astrological sign was Taurus, symbolized by a bull, and Lamborghini made that his cars' powerful logo.

Sports-car lovers were wild about the very first Lamborghini, the 350 GT. They admired its fastback design and V-12 engine that delivered 320 hp. The 350 GT was introduced in

Lamborghini's bull logo was inspired by the company founder's astrological sign, Taurus.

1964, and only 120 were made between then and 1968. In 2005, a mint-condition used model was sold at an auction for more than $315,000!

Lamborghini locked horns with Italian rival Ferrari in the supercar arena in 1966 with the stunning Miura. What made this car especially super was that its V-12 engine was positioned in the middle of the car, just behind the two bucket seats. Most engines are in the front, though some are in the rear.

The Lamborghini Miura was produced from 1966 to 1973, and is very popular with collectors. This is the 1971 model.

While no one could agree whether these so-called mid-engine cars perform better or worse, other carmakers soon followed Lamborghini's lead. Different versions of the Miura were produced until 1973 and today are in great demand by collectors.

Lamborghini turned heads again in 1971 when a prototype, or "concept car,"

WILD FACT

A "fastback" is a car with rear windshield that slopes downward from the back edge of the roof to the rear of the car.

The Dream Machine

The story goes that when a Lamborghini official first saw the new model that was to be shown at the 1971 Munich Motor Show in Germany, he blurted out "Countach!" (KOON-tos). It is an Italian slang word that in English means "stupendous," "magnificent," or "splendid." That was good enough for company founder Ferruccio Lamborghini. He decided then and there that this new supercar would be known as the Countach.

The Lamborghini Countach LP 400

This amazing creation sat wide and low to the ground. It was wedge-shaped, like an airplane wing. The huge V-12, 375-hp engine was in the middle of the car. With the scissor doors opened, the Countach looked like a giant, metallic, winged bug from a science-fiction movie.

In 2004, *Road & Track* magazine called the Countach "a dream machine," even for people who know absolutely nothing about cars.

of its space-age-looking Countach was shown at the Geneva Motor Show in Switzerland. Like the Miura, the Countach influenced the design of other cars during its production years, ending in 1973.

Unlike Ferrari, Porsche, BMW, and its other European competitors, Lamborghini has not concentrated much on racing to develop its supercars. Instead, the company's

WILD FACT

A concept car is a car made by a manufacturer to be a sample of a future design. This design may or may not eventually be built for people to buy.

success is due more to beautiful styling, high technology, and blinding speed on the open road. The latest Murciélago, the LP640, has all of those things. Unlike the earlier version Kobe Bryant was considering, this model offers an automatic option to the stick shift. It is called "e-gear," which the company describes as a "robotized gear-shifting system."

The TR4

- Produced by Triumph Motor Company from 1961 to 1965
- A follow-up to the TR3, a big hit in the 1950s
- The first TR model with roll-up windows instead of plastic curtains
- Special versions with up to 200 hp were successful in Sports Car Club of America races

The 3000 Mark III

- Produced by Austin-Healey from 1963 to 1967
- More luxurious than earlier "Big Healey" models
- Today, a properly restored model can sell for $20,000 to $30,000

CHAPTER 3

Germany's Super Machine: BMW

"The Ultimate Driving Machine" is the slogan BMW uses to describe the high-performance, luxury sports cars it makes at its factories in Europe and the United States. It is worth a test drive in a 2007 BMW M6 to see if it really is the ultimate driving machine.

Imagine a driver cruising along on the famous 7,480-mile German Autobahn. On this highway, there are no official speed limits on many long stretches. What a great place to take advantage of this two-door with a 500-hp, V-10 engine under its sleek hood. Can the M6 really rip from 0 to 60 in only 4.1 seconds?

The accelerator (gas pedal) is pressed to the floor and the M6 takes off like a rocket. The driver's body is pressed back against the leather seat by the force of gravity as those 4.1 seconds fly by. The car hugs the road better than most, thanks to the lightweight carbon-fiber roof and bumpers and its excellent suspension. (The lighter parts toward the top of the car keep its overall weight, mostly from the engine, lower to the ground.)

Instead of changing gears with a clutch and stick shift, the driver can switch between the sports car's seven gears by using a "paddle shifter." It just takes a flip of one of the two small tabs on the steering wheel. The tab on the right shifts the

BMW started off producing motorcycles, then began producing cars in the 1930s. This is a 1937 328 Roadster.

transmission to a higher gear, and the one on the left shifts to lower gears. By the time the car is in seventh gear, the M6 will be buzzing along at 155 mph.

The M6 may be the ultimate BMW, but other BMW models are pretty incredible, too. And that has been the story right from the beginning. The company is located in Munich, Germany. It started out in 1913 by making airplane engines. In 1923, BMW (Bavarian Motor Works) began making motorcycles, for which it is also well-known.

Along with the M models, BMW also offers the 1, 3, 5, 6, and 7 Series vehicles, two different SUVs, and the Z4. The Z4 is BMW's two-seater sports car. It compares to the Audi TT, Mercedes SLK, and Porsche Cayman.

The Z4 is made in the United States, in Spartanburg, South Carolina. It was introduced in 2003 to replace the Z3, BMW's first modern two-seater. The Z4 was only available as a convertible until 2006, when the fastback coupe version came on the scene. The ultimate is the 2007 Z4 M coupe. It has a powerful 330-hp engine and a six-speed manual transmission. It sprints a quarter-mile in 13.4 seconds and can reach a top speed of 160 mph on a closed track. "Fast and furious" is how *Automobile* magazine described the Z4 M after a test drive.

The BMW Z4 M

BMW produced its first cars in the 1930s and 1940s. By the 1960s, it was starting to become well-known in Europe for its sporty-looking, powerful, well-made cars. In the late 1960s, word had spread to the United States. The BMW 2002, released in 1968, became very popular in the United States. The 2002 was compact and fun to drive. It was fast, it handled well, it could seat four, and it did not cost nearly as much as the fancy Italian sports cars.

The first BMW to be popular in the United States was called the 2002, and was introduced in 1968. This is a 1972 model.

Ultimate Two-Wheelers, Too

Like their cars, BMW motorcycles are admired worldwide. The very first model, the R32, came out in 1923. It had a special engine called a "boxer." The boxer featured two cylinders laying flat, instead of straight up or in a V-shape, and opposite each other. This helped to create less engine vibration and a smoother ride. Today's BMW motorcycles still include boxer engines, although the technology has improved a lot over the decades.

The most popular BMW motorcycle today is the R1200RT. It has a big, 110-hp boxer engine that launches the bike up to 125 mph on a closed track. Other features include an adjustable electronic windshield, a two-piece fairing (a fiberglass piece covering the front of the bike), heated seat and hand grips, and a stereo with a CD/MP3 player. It also has amazing comfort, speed, and handling. This ultimate machine can conquer any road.

BMW R1200RT

The success of the 2002 led to the launch in 1975 of the 3 Series. These were high-performance, high-quality cars that put BMW on the path to "ultimate driving machine" status.

The BMW 3 Series has been updated several times since then. One of the best of the 2007 models is the good-looking 335i coupe. The six-cylinder, 300-hp engine will kick the German "wundercar," as *Motor Trend* calls it, from 0 to 60 in 5.1 seconds. And even with a load of options, from heated leather seats to satellite radio, the 335i is a "bargain" at around $46,000—compared to a Ferrari or Lamborghini that can cost ten times as much!

WILD FACT

Horsepower is a measure of engine performance. It compares the power created by one horse to what an engine can do. This means it would take 500 horses working together to produce enough power to drive a BMW M6 at top speed!

CHAPTER 4

Just Say "Wow!": Porsche

If you saw a Volkswagen Beetle parked next to a Porsche, you might not think the cute little "Bug" had much, if anything, in common with one of the world's great sports cars. But you would be wrong! In fact, Ferdinand Porsche, founder of the

You might say that the Volkswagen Beetle and today's Porsches are distant cousins. The first models of both were designed by Ferdinand Porsche, and they shared many of the same body parts.

super-successful car company that bears his name, was an original designer of the first Beetle in 1930s Germany. (The Beetle was eventually built by a new company called Volkswagen, a German word that means "people's car.")

You could say the two cars come from the same automotive DNA. Since that time, the Porsche has gone on to become a supercar all-star—while the Beetle remains a cute little Bug. Both cars are cool and popular, but could not be more different.

J.D. Power and Associates, a company that rates cars every year, ranked Porsche number-one in quality in 2006. The Cayman and Cayman S coupes, introduced in 2006, were major reasons for that praise.

The Cayman S is the more powerful of the two versions. It sports a six-cylinder, 295-hp engine vs. a 245-hp one in the standard two-seater coupe. It turns heads with the fastback design Porsche is known for. On a test drive along Germany's famous Nürburgring racetrack, the Cayman S snaked through the 3.2-mile course's 16 tricky curves in an impressive eight

WILD FACT

For years, people have debated how to pronounce the name "Porsche." Some people say PORSH-uh, while others prefer PORSH. Ferdinand Porsche pronounced his name PORSH-uh. Still, PORSH has always been used, especially in the United States. That is why the debate lives on.

minutes, 11 seconds. On straightaways, it topped out at 170 mph.

The Cayman is one of four basic models currently manufactured by Porsche. The others are the Boxster, the Cayenne, and the 911. All of them are related to the very first Porsche that was sold to customers. Called the 356, it was developed by Ferdinand Porsche's son Ferry and introduced in 1948. Its squatty, roundish design was original. But its four-cylinder engine, suspension, and chassis were largely borrowed from the Volkswagen Beetle. Several versions of the 356 were produced until 1964. Today, collectors pay as much as $100,000 for one of these classic beauties.

The classic Porsche 356 had the same engine and basic body parts as the Volkswagen Beetle. This is a 1954 model.

On the Fast Track

Almost from the time the first Porsche hit the streets in 1948, special racing models have been burning up the world's racetracks.

Porsche racing teams have been most successful in endurance races, which are long-distance events that can last one or more days. Porsche's race cars were winners in the Targa Florio, an endurance race held on the Italian island of Sicily until 1977. After winning the race five times between 1956 and 1964, Porsche named its new 911 model, introduced in 1967, the Targa. After that, Porsche won the race four more years in a row!

Porsche drivers have crossed the finish line first 20 times at the 24 Hours at Daytona event and 16 times at the 24 Hours at Le Mans. That is the most Le Mans wins by any carmaker, by a long shot. Ferrari comes in second, with nine victories.

Porsche Puts the "Vroom" in Harley's V-Rod

Porsche teamed up with Harley-Davidson to develop the amazing engine that powers Harley's V-Rod motorcycles. The V-Rod was introduced in 2001 and was very different from other Harleys. The bike's design was racy and futuristic compared to Harley's other burly cruisers. The V-Rod's engine, though, was the most dramatic difference.

The engine is called the "Revolution." The twin cylinders form a V, but not at the traditional 45-degree angle that Harleys are famous for. Instead, they are at a 60-degree angle, which allows gas and air to mix better in the engine. The Revolution is also the first Harley engine to be water-cooled rather than air-

cooled. The result is an awesome machine that can reach 140 mph on a racetrack. "The thing boogies," is what a review in *Motorcycle Cruiser* magazine stated.

The best-selling Porsche is the 911. First produced in 1964, it is a larger, more powerful version of the 356. There have been many improvements and variations since then. These include the Targa and Carrera versions.

Among the 911s available today, the 911 Turbo is the top of the line. This high-tech two-seater—priced at nearly $123,000—has much of the same styling and mechanics as older Porsches. These include bug-eye headlights and a six-cylinder rear engine.

The best-selling Porsche 911 has been around for five decades. This is a 1996 911 Turbo.

The engine in this 911, though, gives it a huge kick. It has a turbocharger, which supplies more oxygen to the engine. This increases its power. The 480-hp engine in the 911 Turbo can rocket the car from 0 to 60 mph in an incredibly fast 3.7 seconds. On a closed track, it can get up to 193 mph!

In 1996, Porsche introduced the Boxster, a two-door convertible. It was more "affordable" than Porsche's higher-priced models—but still pretty pricey at $45,600. For another $10,000, the 2007 Boxster S features the same 295-hp engine that is found in the Cayman S.

Porsche continues to improve its well-known models. *Car and Driver* magazine reported in October 2006 that the company was developing the next version of the 911, called the GT2. The GT2 will have a slightly different look than the 911 Turbo. It will have a large rear spoiler, plus a 525-hp engine. (A spoiler is a wing-like device that helps a car handle better at high speeds.)

Once you get behind the wheel of a land rocket like this, you might never believe that it is a distant cousin of the tame little Volkswagen Beetle.

With its 420-hp engine, the sleek Jaguar XKR competes with the Porsche 911 and the BMW M6.

CHAPTER 5

Fast and Furious Feline: Jaguar

The British are sometimes thought of as being very proper and polite. England, after all, is known for its kings and queens, who live in stately castles surrounded by neatly kept gardens.

The 2007 XKR from British automaker Jaguar seems to go along with this image—at first. It has a smooth, all-aluminum body, an oval-shaped front grille, and polished chrome exhaust pipes. Inside, there are leather seats and a touch-screen radio/CD player and navigation system.

Step on the gas pedal, though, and the XKR seems anything but proper. On a test track, the V-8, 420-hp engine speeds it from 0 to 60 mph in 4.5 seconds (a V-8 engine is like a V-12, but with eight cylinders). It will dash a quarter-mile in 13 seconds, reaching a not-so-polite speed of 109 mph. This "Jag" is just as much a high-performance sports car as the Porsche 911 or the BMW M6.

Like both BMW and Porsche, Jaguar has a motorcycle connection, too. Jaguar was founded in Coventry, England, in 1922 as the Swallow Sidecar Company. It started out as a maker of motorcycle sidecars (one-wheeled, motorless passenger carriers attached to the sides of motorcycles). The company began making automobiles in 1935. One of its early models was called the Jaguar. The company name was changed to Jaguar Cars in 1945.

This SS100 FHC "Grey Lady" was produced in 1938. That was seven years before the Swallow Sidecar Company became known as "Jaguar."

Jaguar became known for its high-quality luxury sedans, but it has a racy side, too. In fact, the XK120, introduced in 1948, earned that name because of the top speed it could reach (120 mph). It was then the fastest production car in the world. (A production car is one that is made for people to buy, not just as a race car.)

In 1961, Jaguar added the E-Type coupe to its XK line of sports cars. Also called the XK-E, this long, curvy model turned heads in the United States. In its final years of production, from 1971 to 1974, the XK-E turned it up a notch, with a brand-new 12-cylinder engine.

The XJ-S HE made headlines in 1981 as the world's fastest car with an automatic transmission. ("HE" stands for high-efficiency.) It was able to leap to a top speed of 155 mph. But even that model seemed like a slowpoke compared to the XJ220 "supercar" of the early 1990s. This model held the record for the highest top speed of a production car—217 mph! Priced at a whopping $650,000, fewer than 300 XJ220s

The Jaguar XJ220 could reach a top speed of 217 mph— the highest speed of any production car, which is a car built for consumers.

In England, the word "smashing" describes anything very cool and impressive. The Jaguar XK-E was definitely smashing. This model came out in 1961 and was an instant classic. The 1960s was a time of outrageous new style, and the XK-E fit right in. With its super-long front, glass-covered headlights, and disc brakes on all four wheels (which were unusual in those days), it shouted out, "I'm different!"

The XK-E was a rebel under the hood, too. The original version sported a six-cylinder engine that produced 245 hp.

The XK-E's relatively low price tag also made it stand out in the crowd. It cost $6,000 (equal to just over $37,000

The 1963 Jaguar XK-E

today). Ferraris and Lamborghinis, for example, were much more expensive. The entire package—styling, speed, and lower price—made the XK-E a best seller. More than 70,000 were sold worldwide during the 14 years this "groovy" car was made. XKE's are still loved by today's classic-car collectors.

were produced. One was bought by rock musician Elton John.

Jaguar still offers an XJ series, although the newer models are not as sporty as the XJ's of the past. Jaguar also builds several S-Type sedans and two versions of the X-Type, including a Sportwagon with a V-6 engine.

For daring drivers who prefer racier models, the XK Jaguars are the top choice. The XK is a bit tamer than the XKR, but the 300-hp V-8 engine still has plenty of power and speed. England's most popular car magazine, *Top Gear*, picked the 2006 XK as its Car of the Year.

In the end, though, what makes sports cars so much fun is that there are so many different ones to match different tastes. Think of Ferraris, Lamborghinis, Porsches, BMWs, and Jaguars like flavors of ice cream: Is chocolate really better than vanilla? Not if you love vanilla!

For drivers who prefer very expensive, very fast foreign sports cars, the choices are fairly plain. Any one of these fabulous five will do the job very well. But is a bright red Ferrari really better than a bright yellow Lamborghini? Not if you love Lamborghini!

Glossary

accelerator—Formal name for a car's gas pedal, which controls the engine speed.

carbon fiber—Strong, lightweight material used in place of metal on car bodies and parts.

chassis—The "skeleton" of a car, including the frame and wheels that support the car's engine and body.

cylinder—Space inside an engine that contains a piston, valves, and other moving parts that supply power to the transmission, which turns the vehicle's wheels.

endurance race—Long-distance race—either on a racetrack or a course that can cover hundreds of miles—that lasts anywhere from 12 hours to several days.

fastback—Car with a rear windshield that slopes downward from the back edge of the roof to the rear of the car.

horsepower (hp)—A measure of engine performance and power. It compares the power created by one horse to what an engine can do. For example, it would take 300 horses working together to create the same power as a 300-hp engine.

navigation system—Computerized device that uses satellites in space to find locations and map out driving directions.

options—Extra items that are not part of the standard equipment on a car and can be purchased separately. Examples are a larger engine or special wheels.

suspension—A vehicle's system of shock absorbers, springs, and other devices that connect to the wheels to help with steering and make the ride more comfortable.

transmission—A vehicle's system of gears, powered by the engine, that turn the wheels. A manual transmission, often called a "stick shift," requires the driver to use a clutch pedal while changing gears by hand. An automatic transmission automatically shifts gears without the use of a clutch.

Further Reading

Books

Cheetham, Craig. *Supercars: The World's Most Exotic Sports Cars.* Osceola, Wis.: Motorbooks, 2006.

Dredge, Richard. *Concept Cars: Designing for the Future.* San Diego: Thunder Bay Press, 2004.

Frère, Paul. *Porsche 911 Story: The Entire Development History.* Yeovil, Somerset, U.K.: Haynes Publishing, 2006.

Sutton, Richard. *Car.* New York: DK Publishing, 2005.

Internet Addresses

http://www.qv500.com Includes detailed "guides" for every model of sports car.

http://www.scca.com The Sports Car Club of America (SCCA) hosts sports car races and events all over the country.

http://www.seriouswheels.com This site features pictures and information about all kinds of cool cars.

Index

4/08

DEMCO